Landauer Books

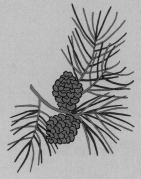

Spirit of the Northwoods
by Debbie Field
for Granola Girl Designs©

Copyright© 2001 by Landauer Corporation
Projects Copyright© 2001 by Debbie Field

This book was designed, produced, and published by Landauer Books
A division of Landauer Corporation
12251 Maffitt Road, Cumming, Iowa 50061

President: Jeramy Lanigan Landauer
Vice President: Becky Johnston
Art Director: Laurel Albright
Technical Illustrator: Mickey Hager
Graphics Technician: Stewart Cott
Photographer: Craig Anderson Photography

All rights reserved. No part of this book may be reproduced or transmitted in
any form by any means, electronic or mechanical, including photocopying,
recording, or by any information storage and retrieval system without permission in
writing from the publisher. The publisher presents the information in this book
in good faith. No warranty is given, nor are results guaranteed.

This book is printed on acid-free paper.
Printed in USA
ISBN 1-890621-31-5

Spirit of the Northwoods

Debbie Field
for Granola Girl Designs©

Introduction

"Nature Is My Spirit"

Each quilt, wallhanging, fabric line, book, or pattern I have designed is a reflection of personal outdoor experiences—inspirations from the breathtaking sights of nature and wildlife. Bringing the outdoors inside by featuring it on a nature-filled quilt offers a warm welcome in almost any room of the house.

I have enjoyed outdoor sporting activities from early childhood into adulthood. My spirit truly belongs to the warmth of my family and living an adventurous outdoor lifestyle.

These experiences that encouraged my love for nature were a gift given and inspired by my parents. I now continue that tradition with my husband, Mark, and our sons, Chad (and wife Jennifer) and Brad (and girlfriend Jami). I am blessed.

Featured on the following pages you'll find 12 blocks for nature-filled wallhangings that can be combined into one spectacular quilt. They offer you the best of both worlds—you can enjoy the great outdoors and quilt it, too!

Debbie Field

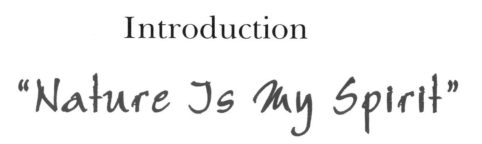

Contents

Special Thanks

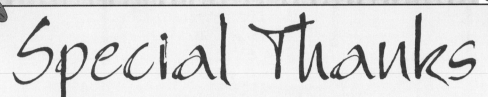

The completion of this book has been made possible with the help of my dependable family, staff, friends, and supply sources:

To my husband Mark—thank you for you never-ending support, encouragement, and countless hours of help, appreciated in every way.

Staff:	Chris Peterson
	Julie Bruss
	Sue Carter
	Delores Farmer
	Sue Longeville
	Trish Mayo

| Machine Quilters: | Cindy's Stitches |
| | All Things Quilted |

Supply Sources:	Troy Corporation
	(Dorothy and Terry Troy)
	Sulky Thread

General Instructions and Helpful Hints

from Debbie Field

Get ready to bring the outdoors in. Hunt down your favorite sewing supplies, sewing machine, small scissors for cutting appliqués, rotary cutter, rotary mat, and two rulers (one ruler should be large enough to square up an 11-1/2" x 11-1/2" block and the other ruler should be approximately 6" x 6" to diagonally cut squares). Choose a variety of embroidery thread colors to match fabric choices. I also recommend a tear-away stabilizer.

Suggested Tools & Supplies

Sewing Machine

Small Scissors

Rotary Cutter

Rotary Mat

11-1/2"x11-1/2" Ruler

6"x 6" Ruler

Embroidery Floss

Stabilizer is placed under the blocks before starting to stitch around the appliqué designs. The appliqué stitch used is a small zig zag setting. Stitch around designs catching the edge of the fabric and covering the raw edge of the appliqué design. Add other stitch choices your machine offers to sew detailed finishing touches on some of the appliqués. For example, refer to the boots, snowshoe, and fly fisherman diagrams. After completing the appliqué stitching and the detailed work, flip the block over to wrong side of block and tear away the stabilizer (following manufacturer's instructions). It is easier to appliqué around the designs on each block before the borders are added, especially if you choose to assemble the large 12-block quilt. **NOTE**: Borders, however, should be first sewn in place and then the border appliqués added.

If you prewash your fabrics you may want to purchase extra fabric to allow for shrinkage. Patterns for the appliqués on the projects in this book were made using unwashed fabrics.

Unless otherwise stated, 1/4" seam allowances are used throughout this book. Please read all instructions before getting started. **NOTE:** Seam allowances are included in the cutting instructions. Check your sewing machine accuracy for the 1/4" seam allowance before starting projects.

Press seams toward the darkest fabric. For small pieces, press in the direction that creates less bulk, making it easier to quilt by hand or machine.
Square up fabric at all times before cutting strips and borders. (A good rule of thumb is to square up your fabric after cutting three to four strips off it.) It is important to align your ruler accurately when diagonally cutting squares into triangles.

One last tip: A clean, oiled machine in good working order takes all the frustration out of quilting and prevents major problems. You should also change your needle after 8 hours of sewing time. When did you last have your sewing machine tuned up?

Appliqués

Appliqué designs are already reversed and will face the direction as photo or diagram shows, unless stated to reverse the design in the instructions.

On the paper side of fusible web, trace around the appliqué designs with a fine tip pencil or marker. **DO NOT CUT** on exact traced line but cut 1/4" **outside** of traced line and position film side down onto wrong side of appliqué fabric choices. Follow manufacturer's instructions on the ironing temperature. Fuse, let cool, and cut out the designs on the traced lines. Remove paper backing and with film side down, position appliqué pieces in place on the appropriate block. **NOTE:** Do not iron appliqués down until <u>all pieces</u> are in place. Stand back to review one last time before fusing in place. (Again, refer to manufacturer's instructions for pressing temperature.)

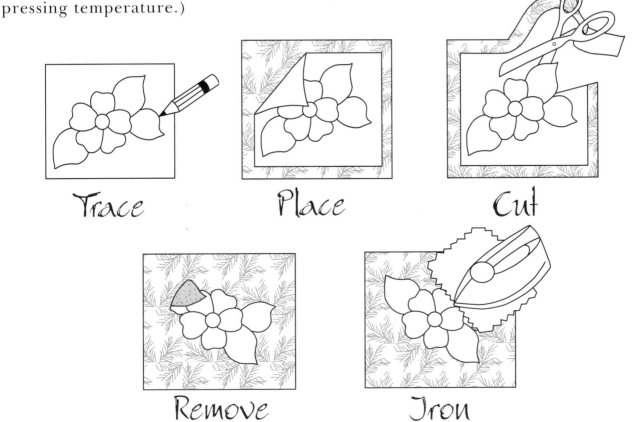

Trace   Place   Cut

Remove   Iron

Spirit of The Northwoods

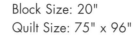

Materials

Fabrics Needed for Each Wallhanging Block

1/3 yard - sky

1/3 yard - ground

1/4 yard large triangles around center

1/8 yard light triangle/square units

1/8 yard dark triangle/square units

1/4 yard outside border

1/3 yard Heat N' Bond® Light

Lightweight Tear-away Stabilizer

2/3 yard Backing

24" x 24" - Batting

1/4 yard - Binding

Sulky Appliqué Thread:
Green, Brown, Black, White,
Gold, Gray, Tan, to match fabrics.

Block Size: 20"
Quilt Size: 75" x 96"

Fabrics are based on 42" wide fabric that has __not__ been washed. Please purchase accordingly.

Materials Needed for Appliqué:

You will need fabric scraps of the following for each block:

January
White for snow; Medium Brown for tree trunks, branches, cabin, & pine cones; Gray Brown for roof; Dark Green for tree boughs & pine boughs; Dark Brown for chimney

February
White for snow; Gray Brown for mountains; Light Green for trees; Dark Green for trees; Light Brown for snowshoes

March
Medium Green for tree boughs; Medium Brown for tree trunks; Light Brown for paws; Black for bear; Gold for bear nose

April
Light Green for bushes; Light Brown for trees & moose antlers; Dark Green for bushes; Medium Brown for female moose; Dark Brown for bull moose

May
Light Gray for pussywillow buds; Brown for tree; Black for chickadee; White for chickadee; Gold for chickadee beak; Medium Gray for chickadee body; Gray/Brown for chickadee wing; and Green for leaf buds

June
Dark Brown for fishing pole, rocks, & creel trim; Medium Brown for rocks & log ends; Light Brown for creel; Gray/Brown for log; Medium Green for tree line; Dark Green for shirt; Light Green for waders; Gold for vest; Tan for face & hands; Light Blue for water; White for water ripple

July
Medium Brown for tree trunks and boot trim; Gold for Boots; Black for boot soles; Dark Brown for land; Dark Green for medium & large trees and treeline; Light Green for small tree, and Blue for river

August

Light Green for small treeline; Medium Green for cattails and bushes; Dark Green for tall treeline; Gold for cattail heads; Medium Blue for water ripple; White for loon chest; 2 Blacks for loon; Black/White for loon wing

September

Light Green for bushes; Dark Green for mountain and bush; White for ducks; Light Gray for ducks; Black for ducks; Gray/Brown for duck wings; Dark Brown for duck wing

October

Light gold for corn stalks; Medium Green for bush; Dark Green for bushes and pheasant head; Light Green for pheasant back; Gray/Brown for pheasant body; Gold for pheasant beak and feet; Fall Print for pheasant wing

November

White for deer chest; Dark Brown for tree trunks; Light Brown for small deer; Dark Brown for large deer; Medium Green for center tree; Dark Green for rest of trees; and a Fall Print for ground cover

December

Gray-Brown for birdhouse; Medium Brown for tree branch, birdhouse logs, and pine cones; Light Green for tree on birdhouse; Dark Green for pine sprigs; White for snow; 2 Reds for cardinal's body & wing; Black for cardinal's and birdhouse hole; Gold for cardinal beak

Cutting Instructions for each Block:
(wof= width of fabric)

Sky Fabric (Center Triangle Top):
- Cut 1 strip 8-1/8" x width of fabric (wof). Recut into 1 square 8-1/8" x 8-1/8". Diagonally cut once for 2 triangles.

Ground Fabric (Center Triangle Bottom):
- Cut 1 strip 8-1/8" x wof. Recut into 1 square 8-1/8" x 8-1/8". Diagonally cut once for 2 triangles.

Large Triangle Fabric (Large Triangles around Center):
- Cut 1 strip 6-7/8" x wof. Recut into 2 squares 6-7/8" x 6-7/8". Diagonally cut once for 4 triangles.

Light Fabric (Triangle/Square Units):
- Cut 1 strip 2-1/2" x wof. Recut into 12 squares 2-1/2" x 2-1/2". Diagonally cut each once for 24 triangles. Cut 4 squares 2-1/8" x 2-1/8".

Dark Fabric (Triangle/Square Units):
- Cut 1 strip 2-1/2" x wof. Recut into 12 squares 2-1/2" x 2-1/2". Diagonally cut each once for 24 triangles.
- Cut 1 strip 2-1/8" x wof. Recut into 4 rectangles 2-1/8" x 1-1/2".

Border Fabric:
- Cut 2 strips 3-1/2" x wof.

Binding (1 wallhanging):
- Cut 2 strips 2-1/2" x wof.

Materials
Fabrics Needed for 12-Block Quilt

12-Pieced and Appliquéd Blocks
1/8 yard Cornerstones

1-1/8 yards Sashing & First Border

1-1/2 yards Second Border

For Border Appliqué

1/2 yard - Green pine sprigs

1/8 yard - Brown pine cones

1/4 yard - Brown branches

6 yards - Backing

Queen size Batt

1 yard - Binding

Cutting Instructions for 12-Block Quilt:

Sashing:
- Cut 9 strips 2" x wof. Recut into 17 strips 2" x 20".

Cornerstones:
- Cut 1 strip 2" x wof. Recut into 6 squares 2" x 2".

First Border:
- Cut 9 strips 2" x wof.

Second Border:
- Cut 9 strips 5-1/2" x wof.

Binding:
- Cut 9 strips 3" x wof.

Piecing Instructions:

(1/4" seam allowances used throughout unless stated otherwise.)

Step 1   With right sides together, sew sky triangle and ground triangle together as shown in Diagram 1. Press seam towards the darkest fabric.

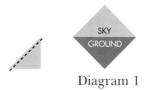

Diagram 1

Step 2   IMPORTANT, PLEASE READ CAREFULLY! Piece your "Floating Block" by placing opposite corner triangles over center square unit (Sky & Ground) as shown in Diagram 2, matching the center of the triangles to the center of the side of the unit. Press. Repeat once for remaining corner triangles. Carefully square up "Floating Block" to an 11-1/2" x 11-1/2" square, leaving a 1/2" allowance beyond the center square unit at the intersecting points. This causes the center unit to "float" as shown in Diagram 3.

Diagram 2

Diagram 3

Triangle Border:

Step 3   Sew one light and one dark triangle together, press and square up. You will have 24 triangle square units. With these units, sew 4 of Unit A strips as shown, and 4 of Unit B as shown, press.

Unit A   Unit B

Step 4   Sew a 1-1/2" x 2-1/8" rectangle between Unit A and Unit B as shown, press. You will need 4 of these Unit C's.

Unit C

Step 5   Taking 2 of the above units sew a 2-1/8" square of light fabric on each end of the above Unit C's to make Unit D as shown, press. You will need 2 Unit D's.

Unit D

Step 6   Sew 1 Unit C to top and 1 Unit C to bottom of the "Floating Block", as shown in Diagram 4. Press.

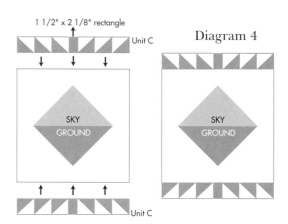

Diagram 4

Step 7   Sew 2 Unit D's onto the sides of the "Floating Block" as shown in Diagram 5. Make sure that dark triangle points are facing out. Press.

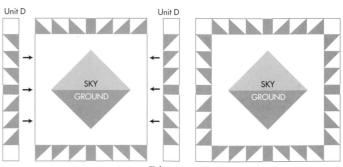

Diagram 5

Step 8 Measure quilt block through the center widthwise for top and bottom border. Cut 2 strips that length and sew onto the top and bottom, press. Measure quilt block through the center lengthwise for side borders. Cut 2 strips that length and sew onto the sides. Press.

Step 9 Follow manufacturer's instructions for fusing fabrics to web. Follow pattern placement for fusing appliqué pieces onto quilt block. Zigzag around each shape.

Step 10 (WALLHANGINGS ONLY) Layer quilt top, batting and backing and quilt as desired.

Step 11 BINDING: Diagonally sew strips together end to end. With wrong sides together, fold strip in half lengthwise and press. Align raw edges of binding to raw edges of quilt top and stitch in place. Turn folded edge of binding to back of quilt top and hand stitch in place.

Assembly for 12-Block Quilt:

Repeat steps 1–9 to make 12 wallhangings. Keep in mind that your choice in sashing fabric should have a calming effect that frames each block to showcase your appliqué work and ties the whole quilt together. (I chose a tiny plaid which reads as a solid.)

Step 12 Sew Sashing strips onto each side of February, May, August, and November wallhangings.

Diagram 6

Step 13 Sew Blocks together into rows as shown in Diagram 7. Press each row in the opposite direction for easier matching of Blocks.

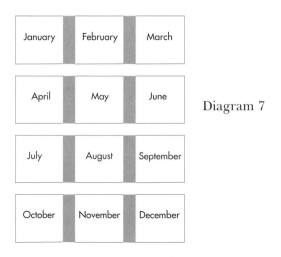

Diagram 7

Step 14 Sew Sashing strips and Cornerstones together as shown in Unit E. You will need 3 Unit E rows.

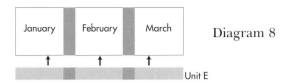

Unit E

Step 15 Sew rows and Sashing strip rows together as shown in Diagram 8. Press.

| January | February | March |

Diagram 8

Unit E

Step 16. Sew the border strips together end to end. Measure quilt top through the center widthwise for top and bottom border. Cut two strips to that measurement. Sew to top and bottom of quilt top and press.

Step 17 Measure quilt top through the center lengthwise for side borders. Recut remaining border strip into two strips of that measurement. Sew to each side of quilt top and press.

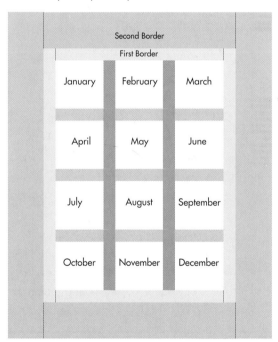

Diagram 9

Step 18 Repeat steps 16–17 for Second Border as shown in Diagram 9.

Step 19 Cut your 6 yards of backing fabric in half to make 2, 3-yard lengths. Trim off selvage edge and seam together lengthwise to make your backing approximately 84"x108".

Step 20 Layer quilt top, batting, and backing and quilt as desired. Bind quilt as stated in Step 11.

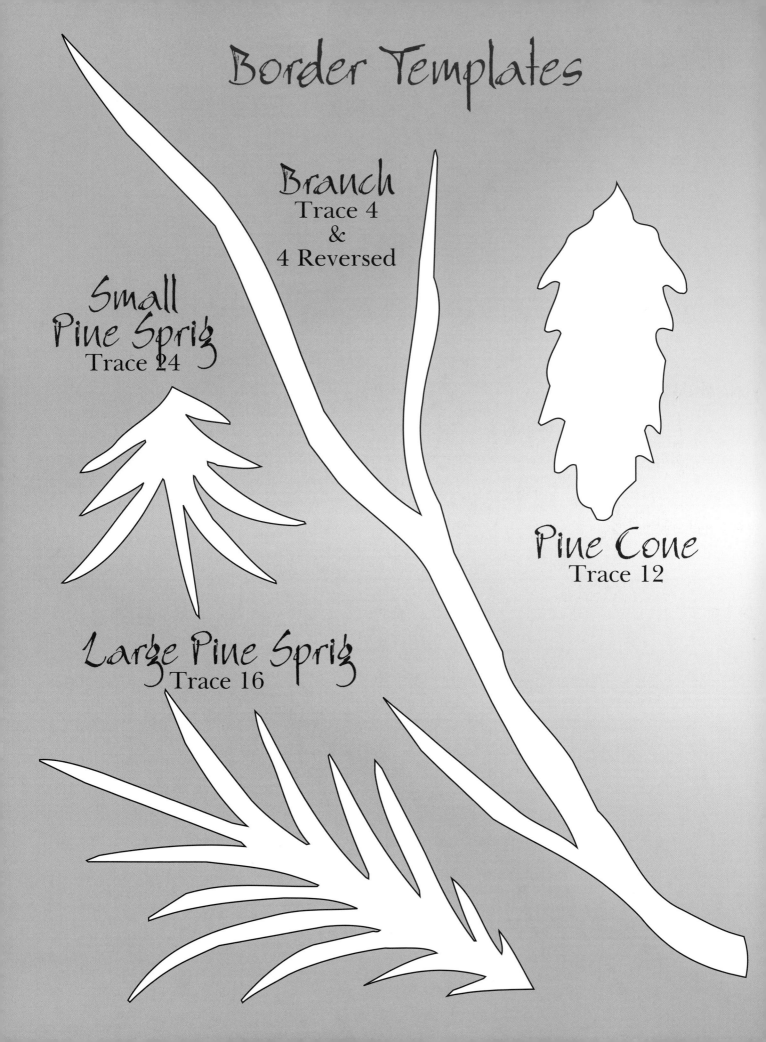

Border Templates

Branch
Trace 4
&
4 Reversed

Small
Pine Sprig
Trace 24

Pine Cone
Trace 12

Large Pine Sprig
Trace 16

Layout for
12-Block Quilt
Border

Repeat for each
corner of border

January

This brings back memories of our cozy

cabin in the winter...

Cabin Comfort

Spirit of the Northwoods

Cabin
Comfort
Diagram

20

Log Cabin Templates

Roof Peak
Trace 1

Chimney
Trace 1

Snow on Roof
Trace 1

Logs Above Door
Trace 1 Each

Roof
Trace 1

Side of Door
Trace 1

Door
Trace 1

Logs
Trace 1 Each

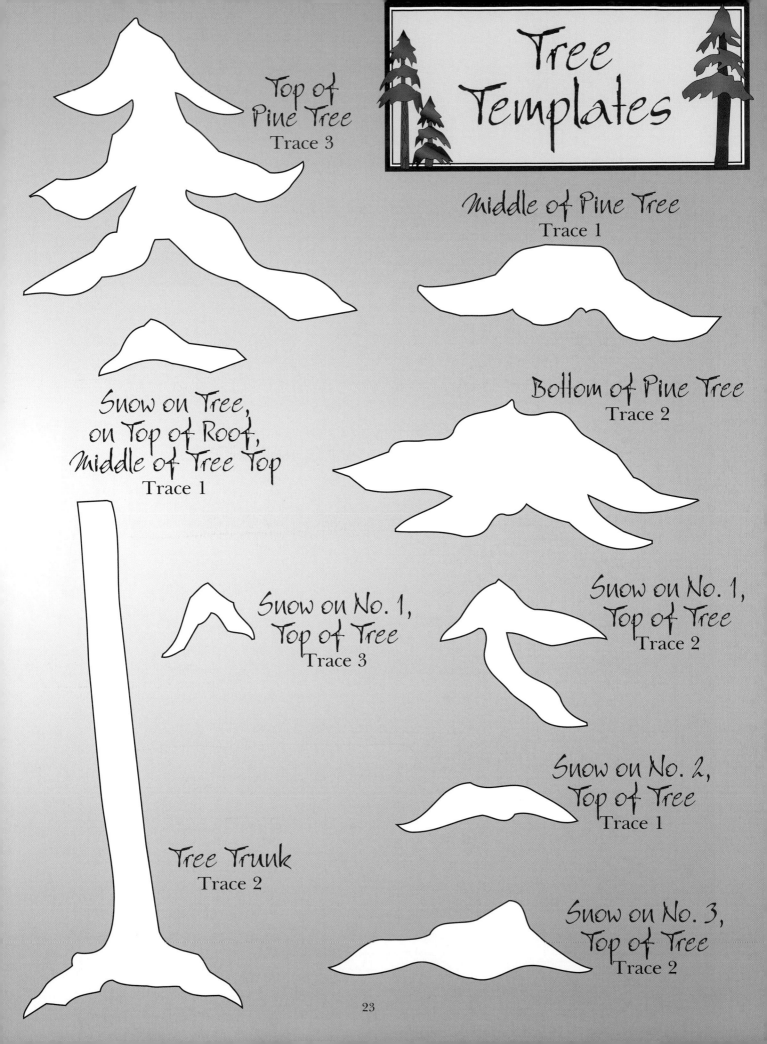

Top of
Pine Tree
Trace 3

Tree
Templates

Middle of Pine Tree
Trace 1

Snow on Tree,
on Top of Root,
Middle of Tree Top
Trace 1

Bottom of Pine Tree
Trace 2

Snow on No. 1,
Top of Tree
Trace 3

Snow on No. 1,
Top of Tree
Trace 2

Snow on No. 2,
Top of Tree
Trace 1

Tree Trunk
Trace 2

Snow on No. 3,
Top of Tree
Trace 2

23

Evergreen Branch Diagram

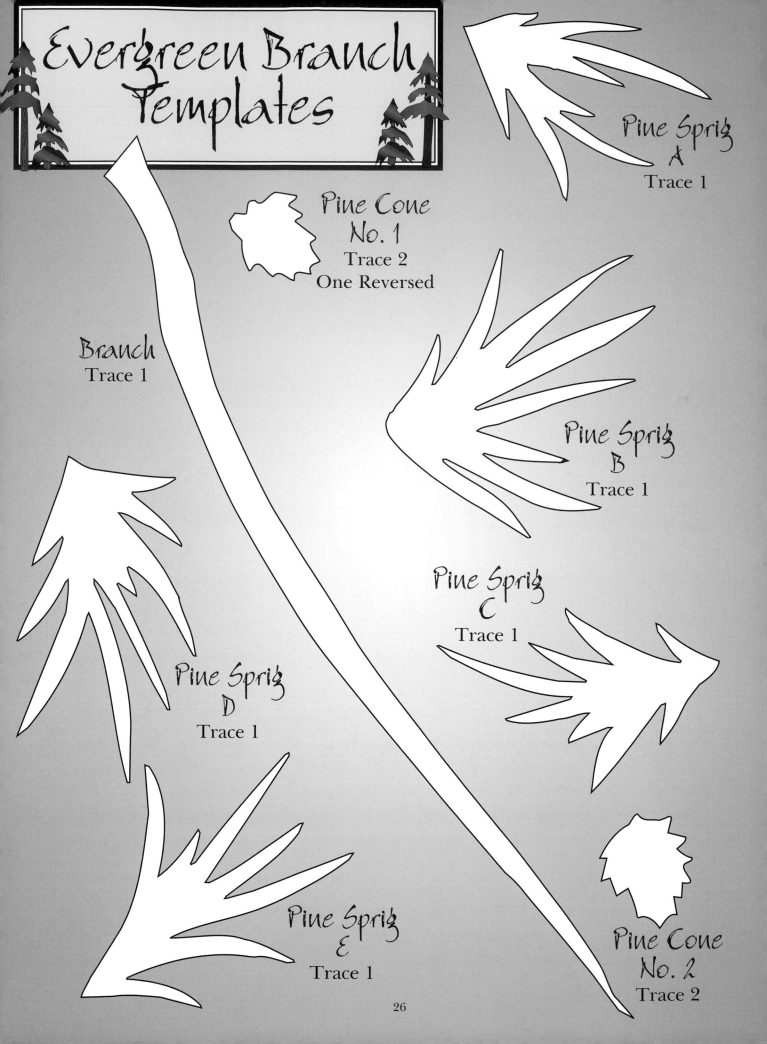

Evergreen Branch Templates

Pine Sprig
A
Trace 1

Pine Cone
No. 1
Trace 2
One Reversed

Branch
Trace 1

Pine Sprig
B
Trace 1

Pine Sprig
C
Trace 1

Pine Sprig
D
Trace 1

Pine Sprig
E
Trace 1

Pine Cone
No. 2
Trace 2

Cabin Comfort

This brings back memories of our cabin in the winter.
After spending the day outdoors in the crisp cold air,
we found the smell and warmth from the fire
burning brightly in the fireplace a welcome treat.

February

There's nothing quite like the
sound of snowshoes breaking the top
crusty layer of snow...

Winter Solitude

Spirit of the Northwoods

Winter
Solitude
Diagram

Mountain Templates

Mountain
Trace 1

Mountain Snow
Trace 1

Tree Templates

Short Tree,
Left Side
Trace 1

Short Tree,
Right Side
Trace 1

Tall Tree Line,
Left Side
Trace 1

Tall Tree Line,
Right Side
Trace 1

Snowshoe Templates

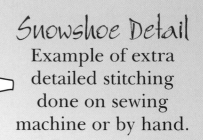

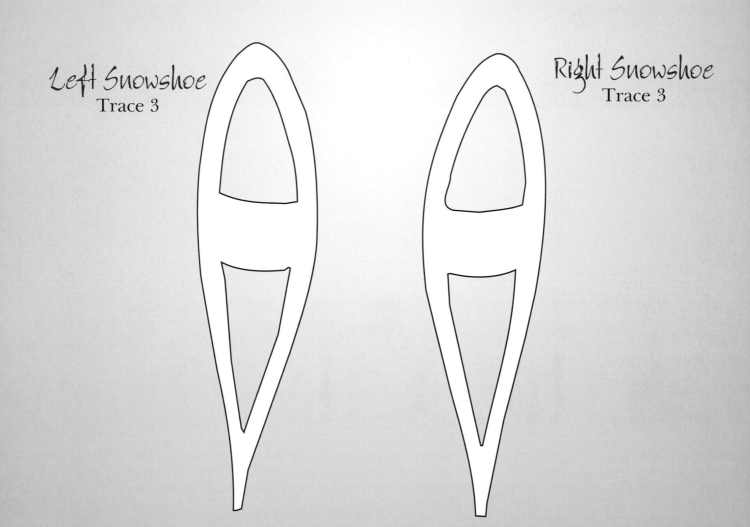

Snowshoe Detail
Example of extra detailed stitching done on sewing machine or by hand.

Left Snowshoe
Trace 3

Right Snowshoe
Trace 3

Winter Solitude

Wherever Mark and I are snowshoeing, whether in the mountains of
Montana or in Wisconsin where we live, there's nothing quite like
hearing the sound of snowshoes breaking the top crusty layer of snow
and enjoying the scenery on a day's outing.

March

We've seen plenty of bears in the

boundary waters on canoe trips and on

our hikes in the mountains of Montana.

Bear Tracking

Spirit of the Northwoods

Bear Tracking Diagram

38

Tree Templates

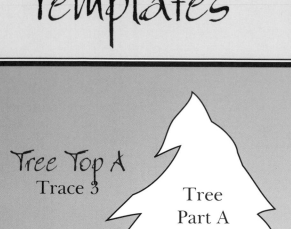

Tree Top A
Trace 3

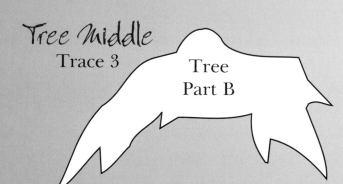

Tree
Part A

Tree Middle
Trace 3

Tree
Part B

Tree Bottom
Trace 3

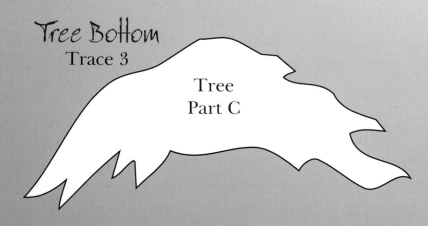

Tree
Part C

Tree Trunk
Trace 3

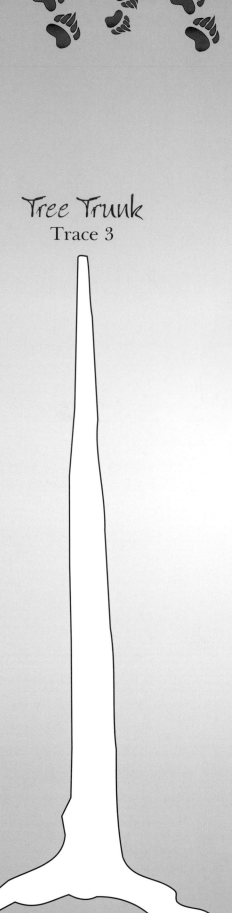

Black Bear
Trace 1

Bear Nose
Trace 1

Bear Prints
Trace 2 Sets

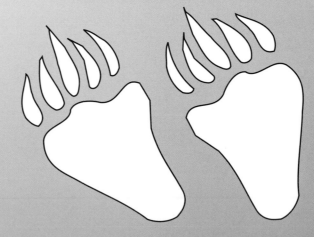

Bear Stitching Templates

Bear Detail

Example of extra detailed stitching done on sewing machine or by hand.

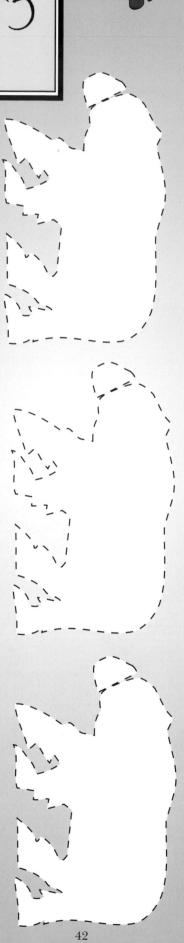

Bear Tracking

We've seen plenty of bears in the boundary waters on canoe trips and on our hikes in the mountains of Montana. One day as we started up a trail head in Montana, we could see in the distance three grizzlies in different spots foraging for food. I quickly decided that we would find another place to hike that day!

April

Moose Meadow, a favorite place to see
moose while cross-country skiing...

Moose Meadow

Spirit of the Northwoods

Moose
Meadow
Diagram

Tree Templates

Tree
Trace 1

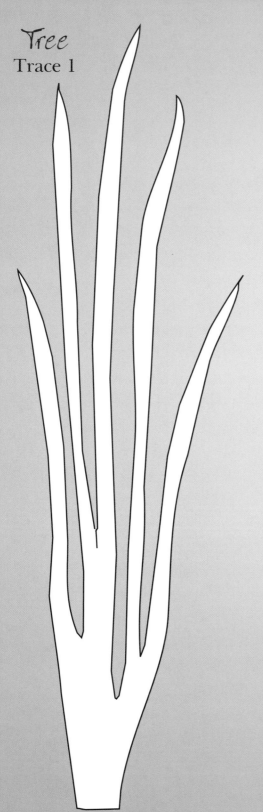

Tree
Trace 1

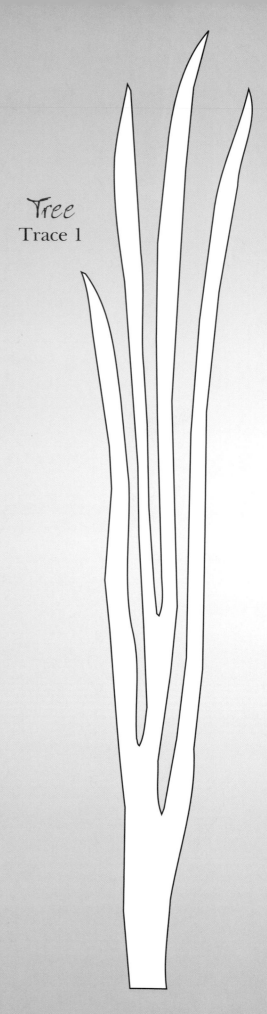

Bush & Brush Templates

Bottom Bush
Trace 1

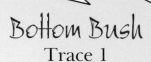

Bush
Background
Trace 1

Bottom Bush
Trace 1

Moose
Antlers
Trace 1 Each

Female Moose
Trace 1

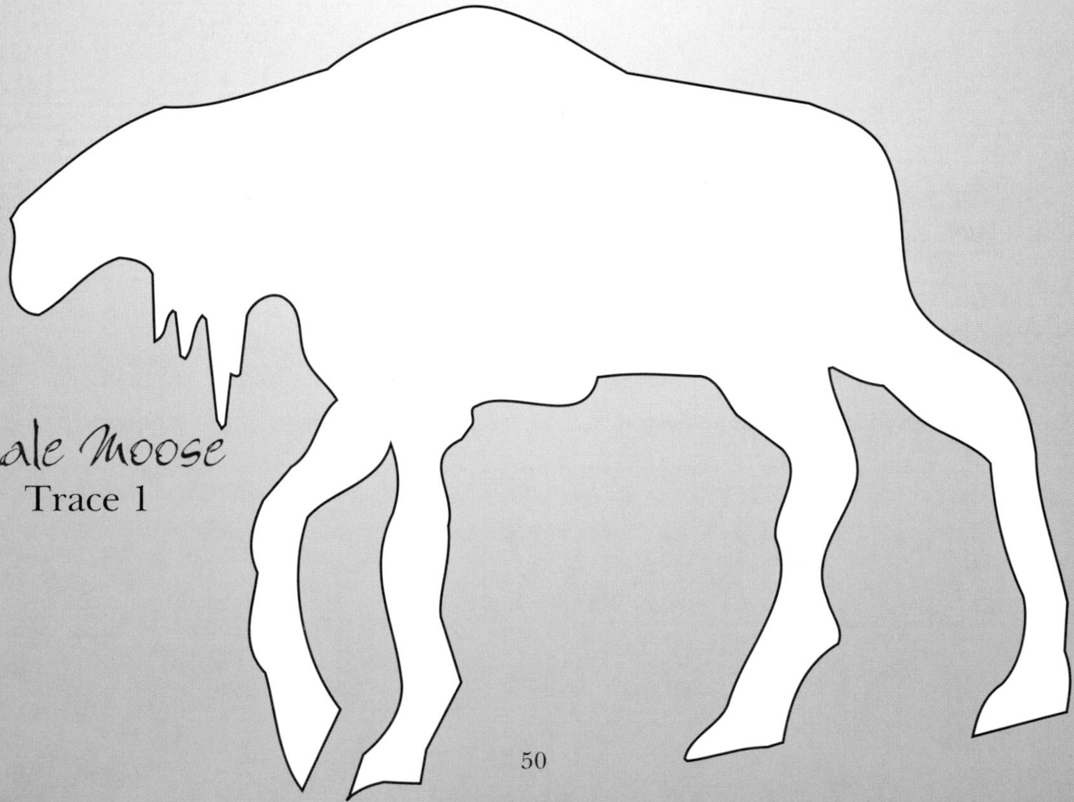

Moose
Templates

Male Moose
Trace 1

50

Moose Meadow

Our favorite sighting place is Moose Meadow, the name we gave to a quiet glen where we often see moose while cross-country skiing. These majestic creatures live deep in the forest and are seldom seen, but when they do appear it is well worth the wait.

May

When my back yard friends come to visit,

I relax with my coffee cup and

take a few minutes to listen to a little

"Chickadee Chatter"...

Chickadee Chatter

Spirit of the Northwoods

Chickadee Chatter Diagram

Leaf
Trace 10

Tree Templates

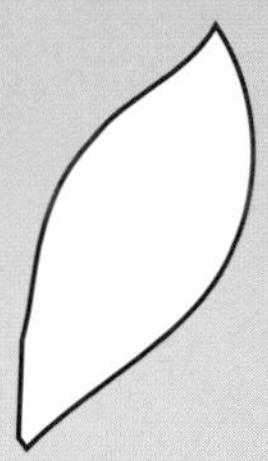

Pussywillow Bud
Trace 24

Branch
Trace 1

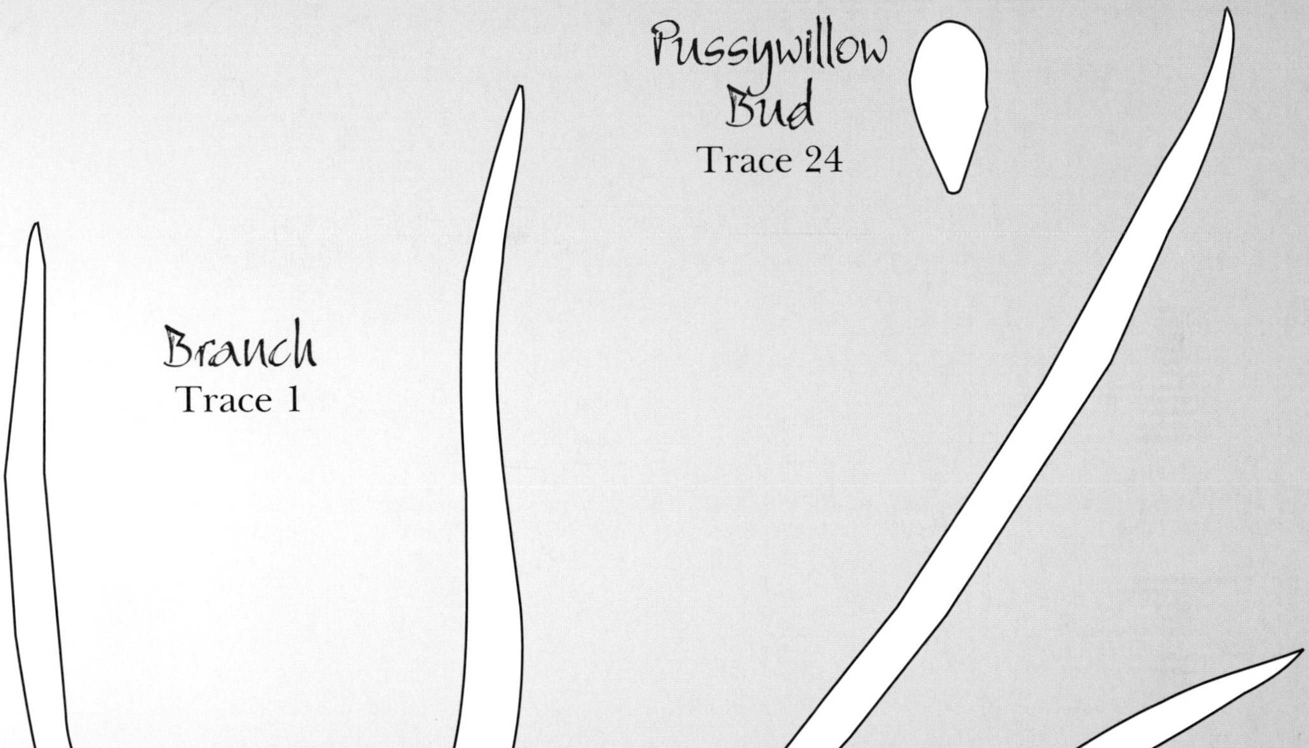

Chickadee Templates

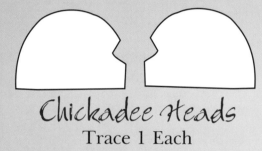

Chickadee Heads
Trace 1 Each

Chickadee Wings
Trace 1 Each

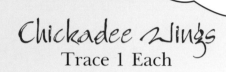

Chickadee Beaks
Trace 1 Each

White Stripes on Heads
Trace 1 Each

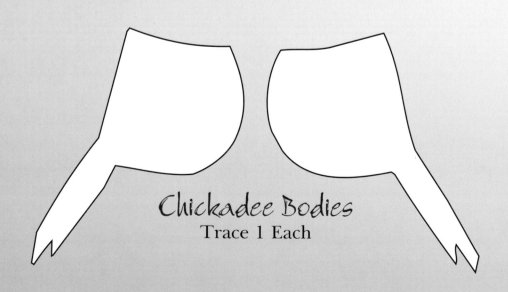

Chickadee Bodies
Trace 1 Each

Chickadee Templates

Flying Chickadee,
White on Head
Trace 1

Flying Chickadee,
Beak
Trace 1

Flying Chickadee,
Head
Trace 1

Flying Chickadee,
Wing
Trace 1

Flying Chickadee,
Wing
Trace 1

Flying Chickadee,
Body
Trace 1

Chickadee Diagrams

Layout Diagram
of Chickadee
on Branches

Layout Diagram
of Flying
Chickadee

Chickadee Chatter

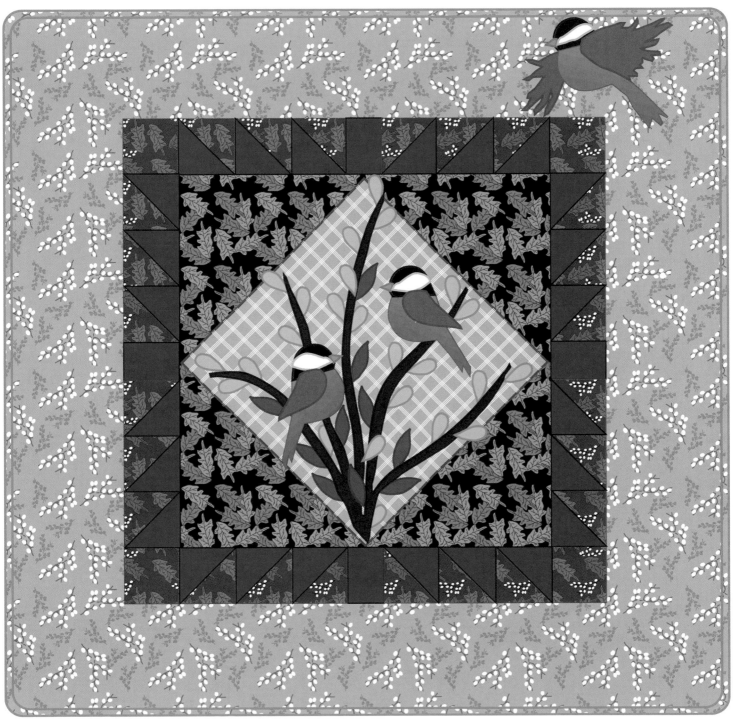

Chickadees are very friendly creatures. I've heard that you can even get them to feed out of your hand with a little encouragement. When my back yard friends come to visit on the first days of spring, I settle back with my coffee cup, coffee pot, and a little "Chickadee Chatter."

June

With fond memories of fly fishing in the ponds and rivers of Montana and Wisconsin...

The Big Catch

Spirit of the Northwoods

The Big Catch Diagram

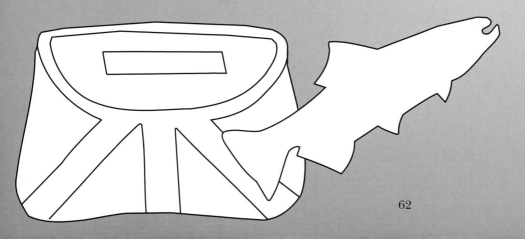

Fishing Creel
Diagram Layout

Creel
Templates

Top Creel Opening
Trace 1

Creel
Trace 1

Creel Trim
Trace 1

Landscape Templates

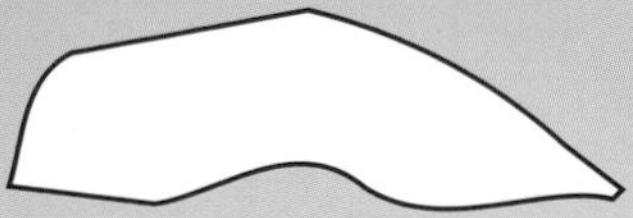

Rock A
Trace 1

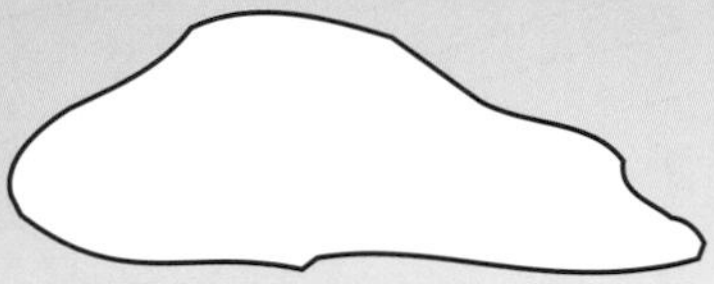

Rock B
Trace 1

Rock C
Trace 1

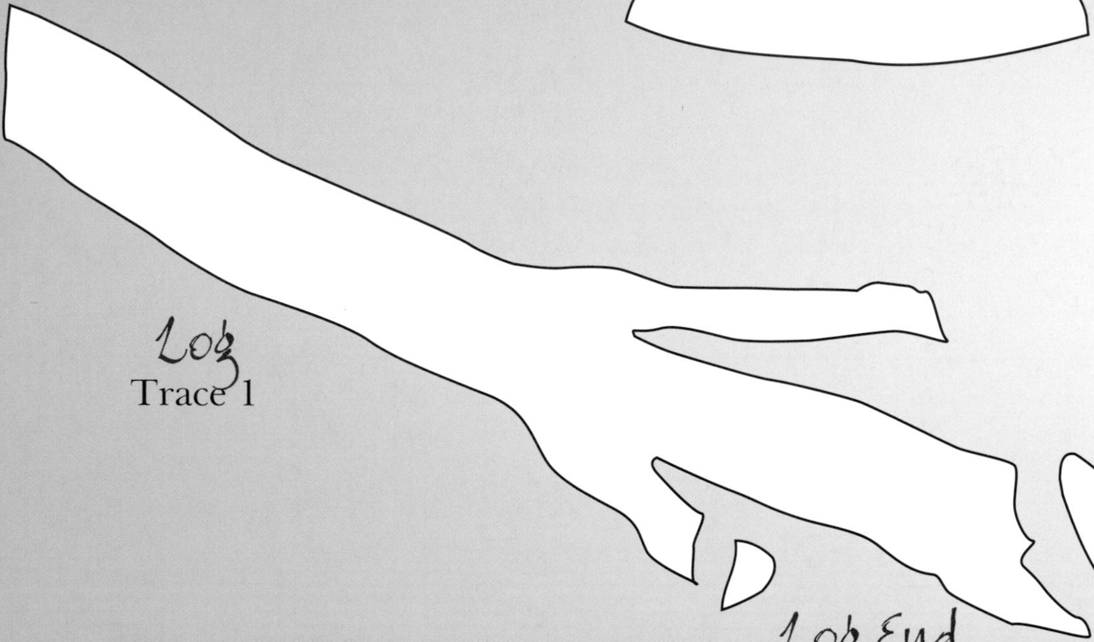

Log
Trace 1

Log End
Trace 1

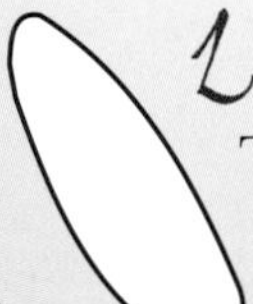

Log End
Trace 1

Tree Line
Trace 1 Each

Fisherman
Face
Trace 1

Fisherman
Hat
Trace 1

Fisherman
Vest
Trace 1

Fisherman
Bottom of Shirt
Trace 1

Fisherman
Waders
Trace 1

Fishing Pole
Trace 1

Fishing Reel
Trace 1

Fisherman Templates

Fisherman
Arm & Hand
Trace 1 Each

Fisherman
Arm & Hand
Trace 1 Each

Fisherman
Layout
Diagram

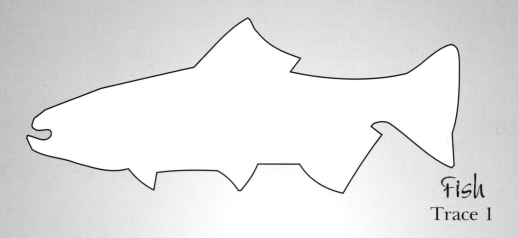

Fish
Trace 1

Water Ripple
Trace 2
1-White
1-Blue

The Big Catch

This handsome fly fishing guy is my husband Mark. We fly fish on the
Gallatin River and mountain lake ponds in Montana and the rivers and lakes in Wisconsin.

July

Hiking boots bring back memories of dipping your tired feet in the ice cold waters of a lake...

Day Hiker

Spirit of the Northwoods

Day Hiker Diagram

Land & Boots Templates

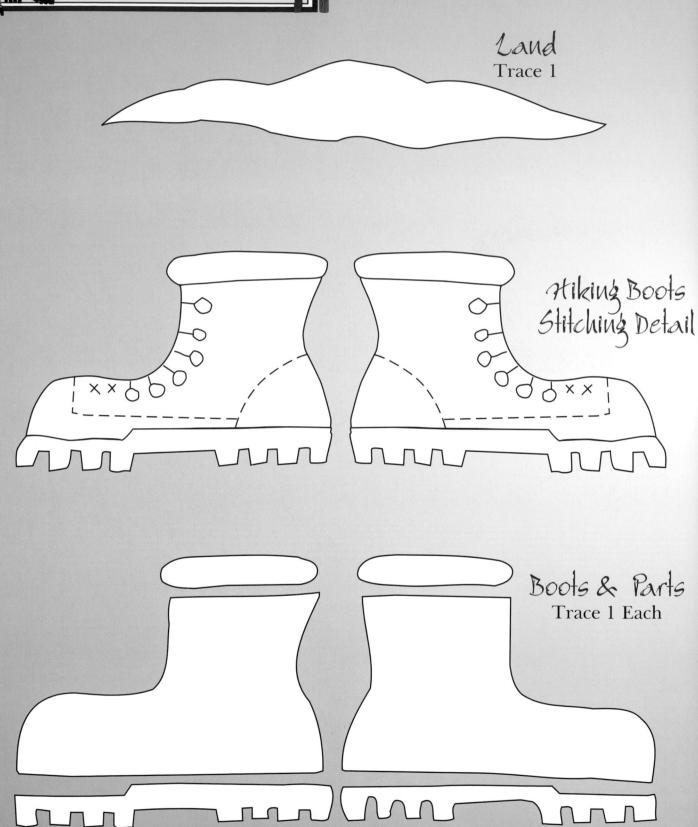

Land
Trace 1

Hiking Boots
Stitching Detail

Boots & Parts
Trace 1 Each

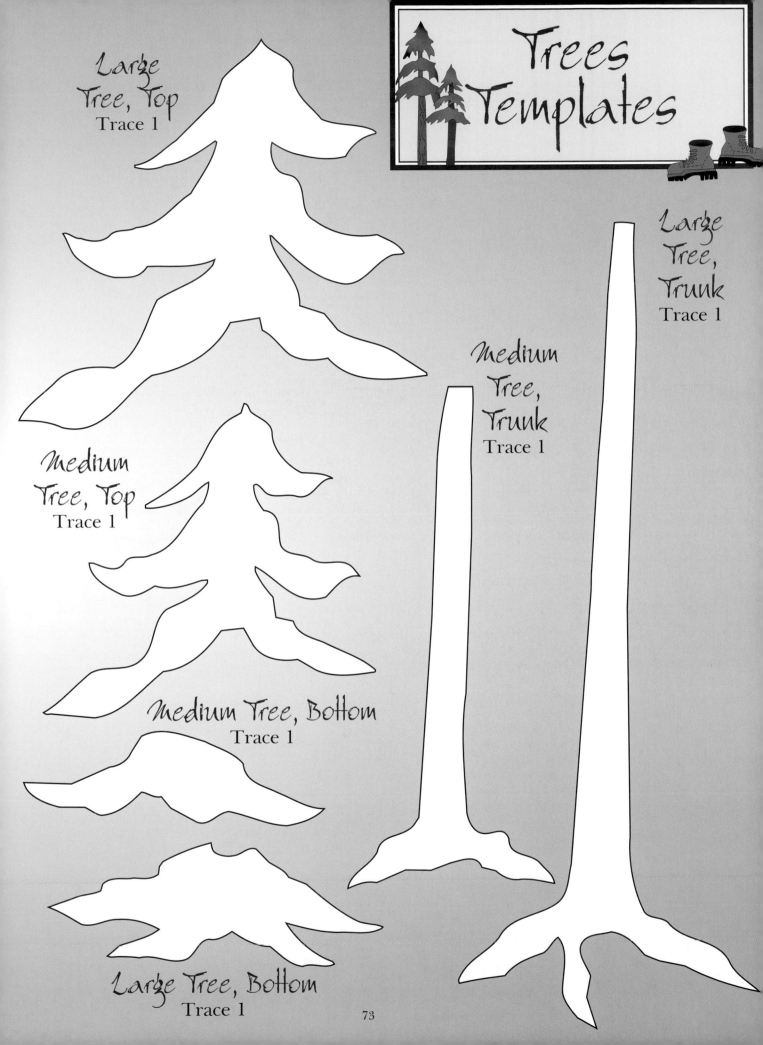

Large
Tree, Top
Trace 1

Trees Templates

Large
Tree,
Trunk
Trace 1

Medium
Tree,
Trunk
Trace 1

Medium
Tree, Top
Trace 1

Medium Tree, Bottom
Trace 1

Large Tree, Bottom
Trace 1

Trees & River
Templates

Small Tree,
Top
Trace 1

Small Tree, Bottom
Trace 1

Tree Line
Trace 1

Small
Tree,
Trunk
Trace 1

Top of River
Trace 1

Position under Tree Line and Land

74

Day Hiker

When we hike a long trail head, we usually head towards a lake or falls or some type of water.
At the end of the trail, my favorite thing to do is take my socks and boots off
and soak my feet in the ice cold water while having lunch—surrounded by nature's sights and sounds.

August

In late summer I enjoy listening

to the haunting sounds of loons

calling to each other...

Loon Lake

Spirit of the Northwoods

Loon Lake
Diagram

79

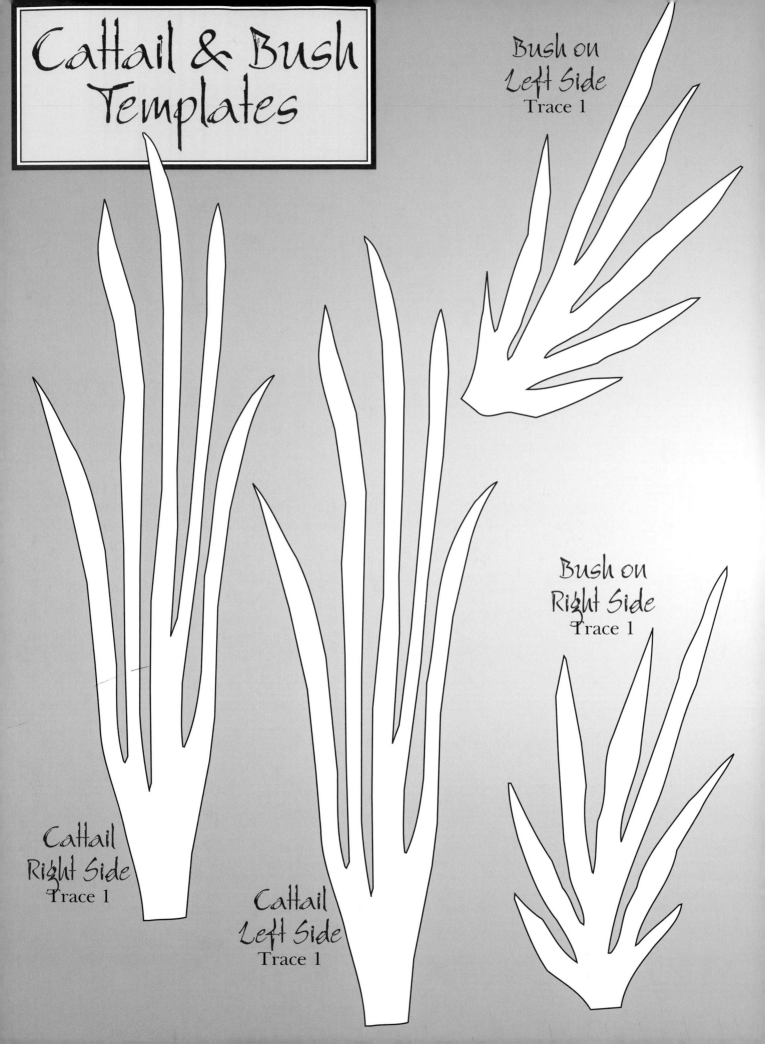

Cattail & Bush Templates

Bush on
Left Side
Trace 1

Bush on
Right Side
Trace 1

Cattail
Right Side
Trace 1

Cattail
Left Side
Trace 1

Loon in
Water Layout
Trace 1

Loon Templates

Loon Neck,
White Part
Trace 1

Loon Head
Trace 1

Loon Wing
Trace 1

Loon Body
Trace 1

Loon Breast
Trace 1

Water Ripple
Trace 1

Bottom Right Loon, Wing
Trace 1

Bottom Right
Loon Layout
Trace 1

Bottom
Right Loon,
Body
Trace 1

White Neck
Pieces
Trace 1 Each

Bottom Right
Water, Ripple
Trace 1

Bottom
Right Loon,
Breast
Trace 1

Cattail & Trees Templates

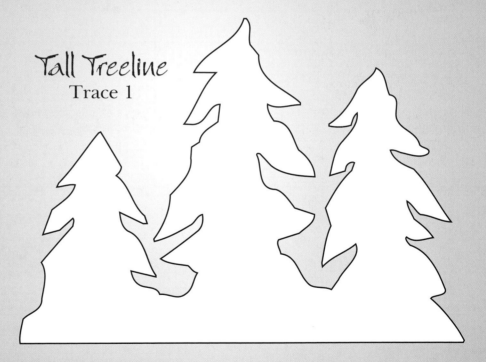

Cattail Heads
Trace all 13

Tall Treeline
Trace 1

Small Treeline
Trace 1

Loon Lake

Whenever we visit Grandma Ruth at her home on the lake, we see loons. I could watch them for hours.
The sounds they make are incredible. I enjoy listening to them "singing" to each other.

September

The leaves on the trees start to turn color and

the geese are getting restless...

Autumn Splendor

Spirit of the Northwoods

Autumn Splendor Diagram

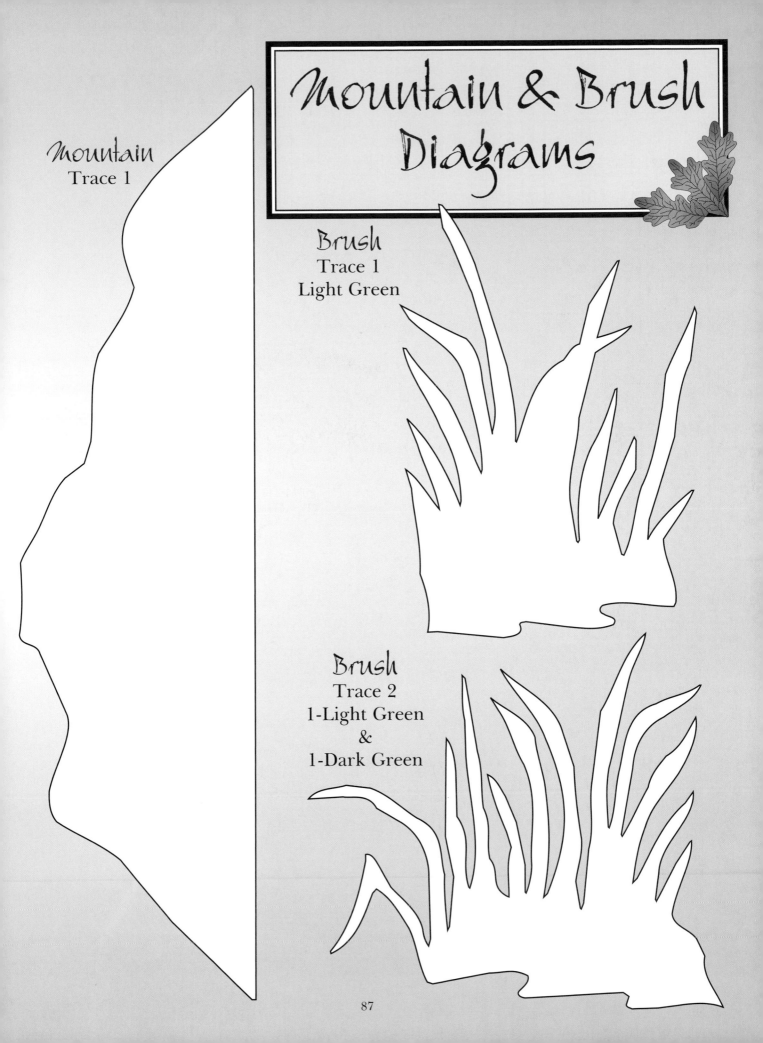

Mountain
Trace 1

Mountain & Brush Diagrams

Brush
Trace 1
Light Green

Brush
Trace 2
1-Light Green
&
1-Dark Green

Goose Templates

Standing Goose, Tail
Trace 1

Standing Goose, White Part
Trace 1

Standing Goose, Head
Trace 1

Standing Goose, Wing
Trace 1

Standing Goose, Feet
Trace 1

Standing Goose, Breast
Trace 1

Standing Goose, Top Wing
Trace 1

Flying Goose, Wing
Trace 1

Flying Goose, Head
Trace 1

Flying Goose, Breast
Trace 1

Flying Goose, Feet
Trace 1

Flying Goose, Tail
Trace 1

Flying Goose, Under-Breast
Trace 1

Fying Goose, White Part
Trace 1

Flying Goose, Back Wing
Trace 1

Flying Goose, Wing
Trace 1

Autumn Splendor

My favorite time of year is when the weather is starting to chill and the geese are getting restless and ready for flight.
The leaves on the trees start to turn color and the woodbox needs to be replenished for lighting fires to warm cool evenings.

October

Pheasant feathers blend almost perfectly

with the leaves and fall landscape...

Nature's Harvest

Spirit of the Northwoods

Nature's Harvest Diagram

Pheasant,
Beak
Trace 1

Pheasant,
Eye
Trace 1

Pheasant,
Head
Trace 1

Pheasant
Templates

Pheasant,
Body
Trace 1

Top of Back

Pheasant,
Back
Trace 1

Pheasant, Feet
Trace 1

Pheasant, Wing
Trace 1

Brush &
Corn Stalks

Pheasant,
Tail
Trace 1

Corn
Stalk
No. 6
Trace 1

Brush Above Pheasant
Trace 1

Corn
Stalk
No. 5
Trace 1

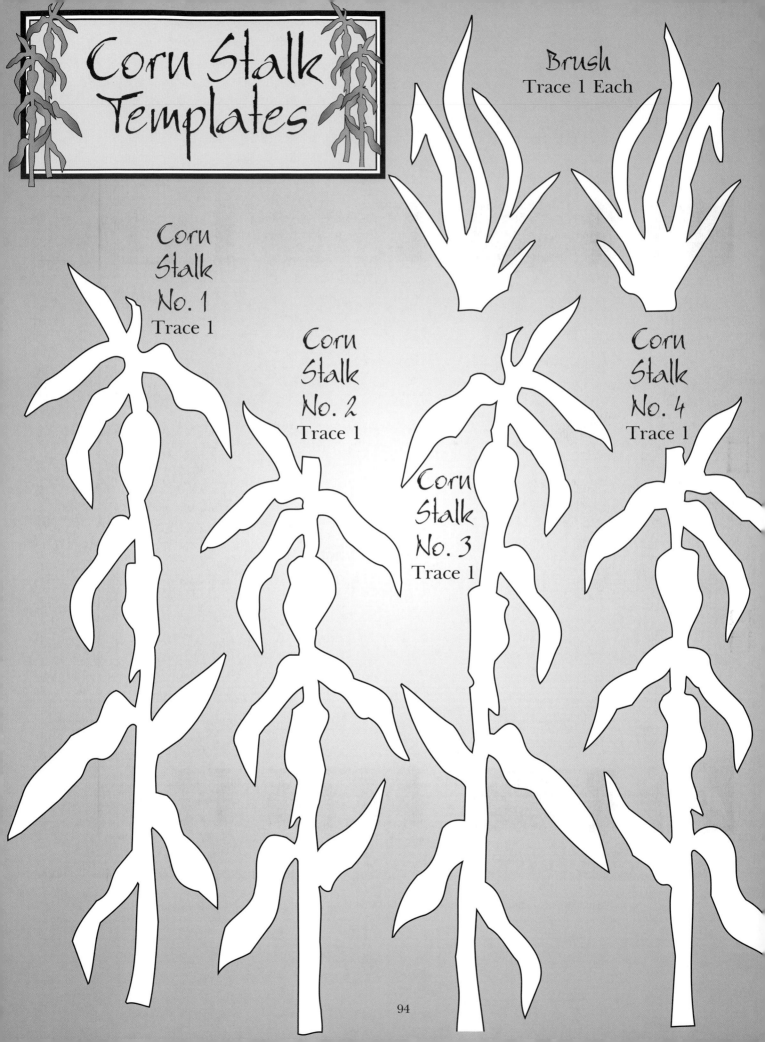

Corn Stalk
Templates

Brush
Trace 1 Each

Corn
Stalk
No. 1
Trace 1

Corn
Stalk
No. 2
Trace 1

Corn
Stalk
No. 3
Trace 1

Corn
Stalk
No. 4
Trace 1

94

Nature's Harvest

Pheasants are checking out the cornfields, plumping up for the bleak winter months ahead.
It amazes me how their feathers blend in so well with the leaves and the fall landscape.

November

A doe and her fawn

make a beautiful woodland pair…

Deer Ridge

Spirit of the
Northwoods

Deer Ridge Diagram

Doe
Trace 1

Neck

Doe,
White Breast
Trace 1

Fawn, Head
Trace 1

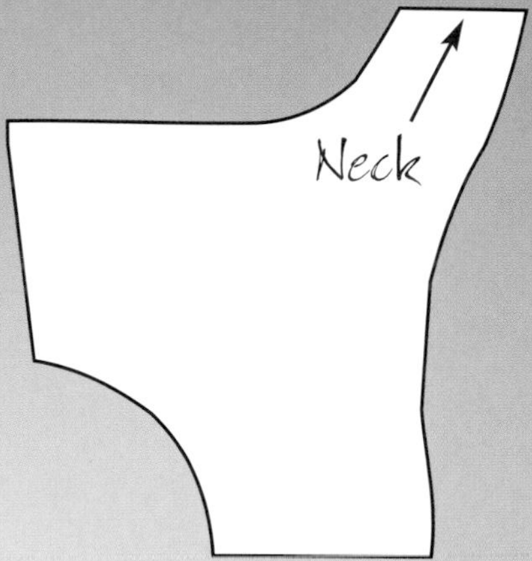

Doe, Body
Trace 1

Doe,
White Breast
Trace 1

Deer
Templates

Tree,
Trunk
Trace 2

Neck

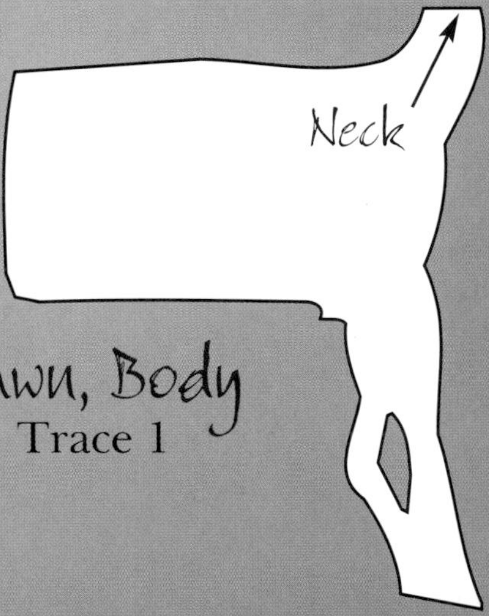

Fawn, Body
Trace 1

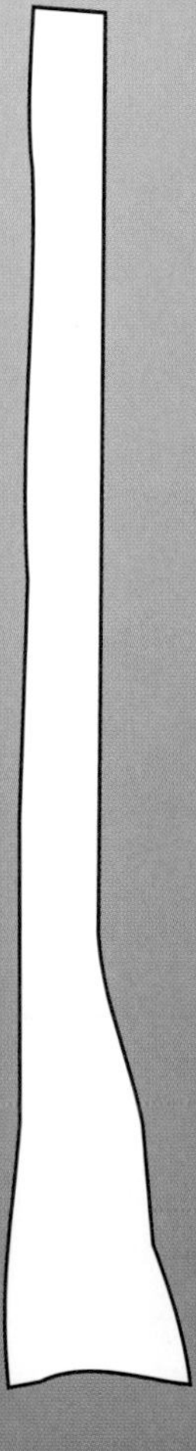

Center
Tree Trunk
Trace 1

Tree Greens Templates

Medium Green
Tree, Top
Trace 1

2nd Part,
Medium
Green Tree
Trace 1

3rd Part,
Medium
Green Tree
Trace 1

4th Part,
Medium
Green Tree
Trace 1

Dark Green
Tree, Top
Trace 1

2nd Part,
Dark
Green Tree
Trace 1

3rd Part,
Dark
Green Tree
Trace 1

4th Part,
Dark
Green Tree
Trace 1

5th Part,
Dark
Green Tree
Trace 1

Deer Ridge

The deer and their fawns have been munching their way through the summer so that they can survive the winter ahead. A doe and fawn make a beautiful pair as they glide almost noiselessly through the forest, disappearing almost as quickly as they appear.

December

I love to see the contrast of the

cardinal's robe of bright red feathers

against the mantel of white snow...

Daily Roost

Spirit of the Northwoods

Daily Roost Diagram

Diagram of Pine Branches Connected

Dotted Lines on
Pine Branch
Part 1 & 2 must stitched
together to make one
continuous branch

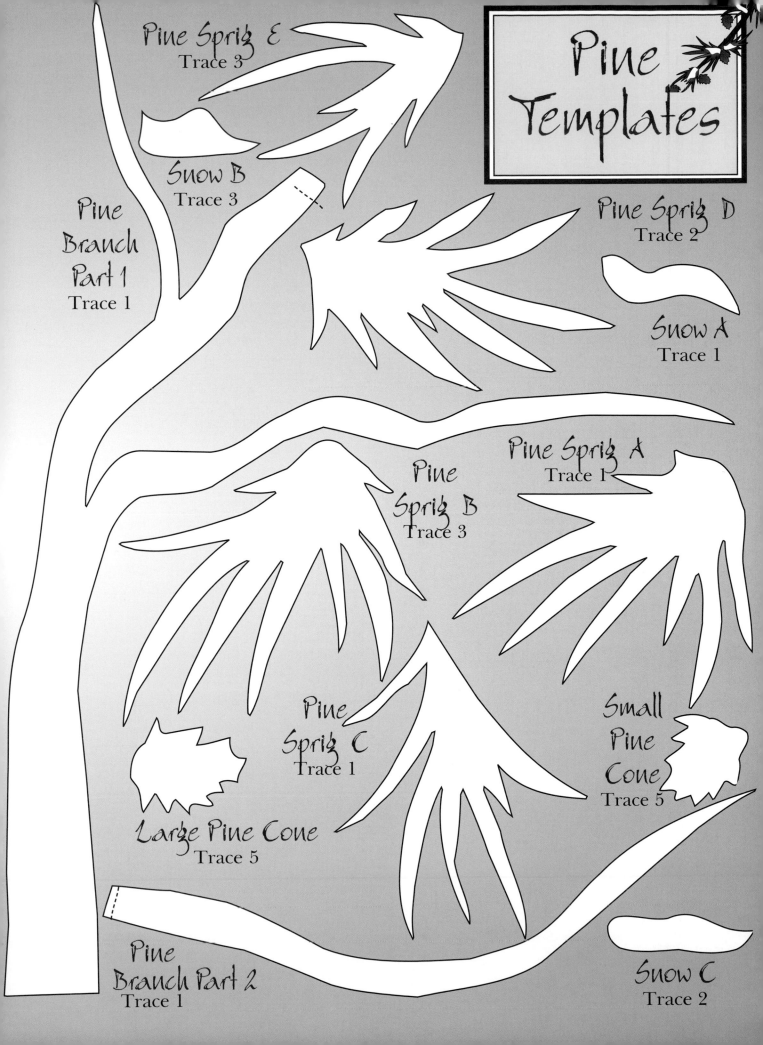

Pine Sprig E
Trace 3

Pine Templates

Snow B
Trace 3

Pine Branch Part 1
Trace 1

Pine Sprig D
Trace 2

Snow A
Trace 1

Pine Sprig A
Trace 1

Pine Sprig B
Trace 3

Small Pine Cone
Trace 5

Pine Sprig C
Trace 1

Large Pine Cone
Trace 5

Pine Branch Part 2
Trace 1

Snow C
Trace 2

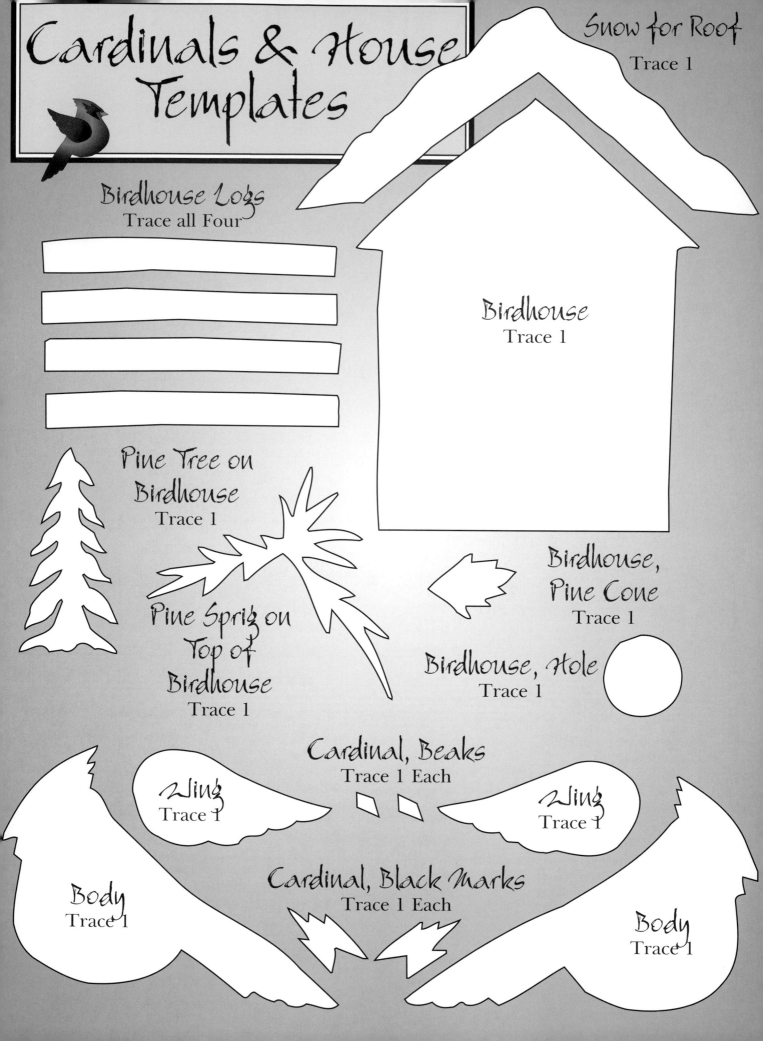

Cardinals & House Templates

Snow for Roof
Trace 1

Birdhouse Logs
Trace all Four

Birdhouse
Trace 1

Pine Tree on Birdhouse
Trace 1

Pine Sprig on Top of Birdhouse
Trace 1

Birdhouse, Pine Cone
Trace 1

Birdhouse, Hole
Trace 1

Cardinal, Beaks
Trace 1 Each

Wing
Trace 1

Wing
Trace 1

Body
Trace 1

Cardinal, Black Marks
Trace 1 Each

Body
Trace 1

Daily Roost

I love watching the birds and feeding them in the winter. Some come on a daily basis, others are only there during certain times of the day. The cardinal, who seems to think he is king likes to come early in the morning to dine before the feeder gets crowded. I love to see the contrast his robe of bright red feathers makes against the white snow.

"All Hung Up"
Quilt Hangers

For more information call
(920) 406-1614
Granola Girl Designs

Bears

Birdhouses

Chickadees

Pine trees

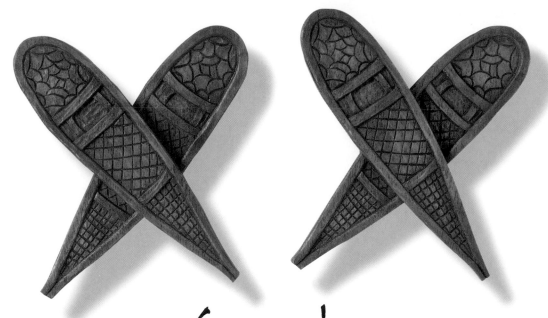

Snowshoes

Leaves

Creel & Rod

About the Artist

Debbie Field, producing her work through Granola Girl Designs, has emphasized her love of the outdoors in quilts, wallhangings, books, patterns, accessories, and her own lines of fabric. Her work is a reflection of her personal experiences since childhood with the breathtaking sights of nature and wildlife of the great northern woods.

She attributes her outdoor spirit to the warmth of her family and living an adventurous outdoor lifestyle—a tradition instilled by her parents and continued with her husband and her sons and their families.